the department of peace

the department of peace

Bonnie Wai-Lee Kwong

SIXTEEN RIVERS PRESS

Sixteen Rivers Press

Printed in the United States of America

Published by Sixteen Rivers Press
P.O. Box 640663
San Francisco, CA 94164-0663
sixteenrivers.org

LCCN: 2024952900
ISBN: 978-1-939639-40-0

Cover and interior art: Glenna Cole Allee
Design: Jeremy Thornton

Contents

fo² 火 fire

Foreword

In *the department of peace,* Bonnie Wai-Lee Kwong's third full-length poetry collection, the author takes the reader on a journey through both historical and personal traumas in which the speaker wrestles with issues of belonging and identity. Kwong uses exacting details, suggestive lyricism, and forms of documentary poetics to let readers interpret for themselves how present-day encounters can be influenced by the legacies of war, displacement, gender-based violence, and pervasive racism.

I met Bonnie in 2018 through Penny Edwards, a professor at UC Berkeley and the producer of a collaborative project entitled "artographies: in other words / worlds." For this project, Bonnie and I worked on a sound collage and text collaboration inspired by story circles with refugees in the SF Bay Area. Four of these pieces are included in this collection.

A poet and playwright who creates in many mediums and languages—English, Cantonese, Mandarin, Japanese, javascript, ASL, and Elixir, to name a few—Bonnie incorporates multilingual knowledge in her work. With an unerring eye, she skillfully weaves together charged political critique, complex family experiences, and meditations on the natural world in poems that compel and reveal.

The book's titular poem, "the department of peace," braids together reflections on the speaker's childhood in Hong Kong and agonizing vignettes of war and the human toll of authoritarianism. This profound collection explores vast territories, both thematic and geographic, while remaining tethered to the poet's experiences as a Chinese American writer, woman, and mother.

With a voice both thought-provoking and poignant, Bonnie Wai-Lee Kwong documents the stories of those who attempt to counter oppression by insisting on our capacity to create interconnectedness across borders and identities. *the department of peace* offers all of us who read her work a space to reckon with and find the means to embody a multiplicity of histories.

—Maw Shein Win

seeds of a cut flower

屈原 qū yuán goes fishing

舉世皆濁我獨清	*In a corrupt world, I alone am pure.*
衆人皆醉我獨醒	*In a drunken crowd, I alone am sober.*
—屈原	—Qū Yuán

have another one on me cheers

how do we say *cheers* in russian

salud 乾杯 *gān bēi* *kanpai*

bottoms up build up your tolerance

you're missing some enzymes bro

don't puke on my shoes these are new

i'm no fisherman no fisherman's wife

i do know how to fish i'll buy you a hook tomorrow

i'll buy you a sink

dig up a worm or two for bait

bring back a fish

to share with some kids

just like everyone else

don't kill yourself

i'm tired of mourning

seeds of a cut flower

easy   as the balance

of books on my head

i walked across the living room

if

the sway of my back

touched a nerve   if

my heels

didn't meet the floor

my mother would hold

the   feather duster

like a whip   welts

the shape of leeches

rose

on

my calves

my mother   sang to me

in three languages

though I've never heard her

sing   in the one

her parents spoke

你問我愛你有多深

nǐ wèn wǒ ài nǐ yǒu duō shēn

我愛你有幾分

wǒ ài nǐ yǒu jǐ fēn

You ask how deeply I love you,

the measure of my love.

i trace the arc

of her scar   from a servant

slamming the door

on her palm

the prune-shaped muscle

under her thumb

my grandmother

stopped walking

to school

when the warlords came

my mother

cleared a

path to college

the way my father

walked in the hills   swinging a stick

to ward off dogs

my mother

wielded

a feather duster a broom

and a spatula

as if she could close

her mind like a book

on

happily ever after

你去想一想

nǐ qù xiǎng yī xiǎng

你去看一看

nǐ qù kàn yī kàn

月亮代表我的心

yuèliàng dàibiǎo wǒde xīn

Think about this *Take a look*

The moon

is a

symbol of my love

輕輕的一個吻

qīngqīng de yīgè wěn

已經打動我的心

yǐjīng dǎdòng wǒde xīn

深深的一段情

shēnshēn de yīduàn qíng

教我思念到如今

jiào wǒ sīniàn dào rújīn

All it took was a light kiss

to move my heart

To this day

I remember this deep love

on the far side

of the moon

unnoticed

i gather

the trim of a coxcomb 雞冠花

gai[1] gun[1] faa[1] *jī guān huā*

i secretly planted

after lunar

new year

from the seeds

of a cut flower

it bloomed for months

unabashed

next to a flowerless orchid

a coxcomb

like the convolutions

of my mother's mind

her housemate in boston

anthrax

in the carpet

orange

alert

yellow

alert

我的情也真

wǒ de qíng yě zhēn

我的愛也真

wǒ de ài yě zhēn

My passion is real

My love is real

my mother

taught me

how to read

before

my baby brother

was born

my books

would watch me   while

she tended the baby

page after page

leaves of books

i asked

how i might touch

the newborn   *anywhere*

gently

was the reply

i touched my brother's

lower lip

there is a lullaby

for boys

月光光照地堂

jyut^{6} gwong^{1} gwong^{1} ziu^{3} dei^{6} tong^{4} 蝦仔你乖乖瞓落床

The moon shines *haa^{1} zai^{2} nei^{5} gwaai^{1}gwaai^{1} fan^{3} lok^{6} cong^{4}*

over the earth *Baby boy,* *be good*

Go to sleep

my mother taught me

this song and more there was no telling

when she was in a mood to sing

when she would pick up

the feather duster

the bathroom was a safe place

i sat in the tub reading

till the water was cold as winter

porcelain

in a faraway i want to return

land this love

measured in welts

月亮 *yuè liang* *The moon*

代表我的心 *dài biǎo wǒ de xīn* *is a symbol of my love*

輕輕的一個吻 *qīngqīng de yīgè wěn* *A light kiss was all it took*

已經打動我的心 *yǐjīng dǎdòng wǒde xīn* *to move my heart*

深深的一段情 *shēnshēn de yīduàn qíng* *This deep love*

教我思念到如今 *jiào wǒ sīniàn dào rújīn* *To this day,* *I remember*

we have the right

to remain on the far side

of the moon

my father once broke

picture frames in anger frames empty

of the cheap art my uncle sold .

to tourists

boats with white sails

drenched in sunset

the fragrant harbor

chinese wigwams

dinner plate shrap

nel

on the kitchen floor the united states

is the country

where julie andrews learned to sing:

my mother imagined *I have confidence in sunshine*

uighurs as criminals

in the golden state

julie andrews never learned

to properly yodel

to the young men

who snatched my mother's purse:

there are

satellite photos

of the far side

of the moon

jointly and severally

there are many

stories

we might tell

unopened

the hoot

of

burrowing owls doesn't

disclose

the borders

of turbines

they've flown

across

there was a book on the shelf

my daughter

would rather not open

a book

about returning to china

an effusion

of colors

once upon a time

my fifth aunt was a child bride

in thailand

she may have lost

her husband

to the thai police

the hong kong police

may have slipped

drugs to my second uncle

in a prison

colonial times the uncle

ran

leftist

meetings

on my

grandparents' farm

my mother

applied for a

government job she didn't get she had to list

all siblings

her leftist

brother the political prisoner

who

never quite recovered

the blanks

the girls

given away

the almanac

warning of

inauspicious

days

when

my grandparents shunned

friends who knocked

on their door

what to avoid

when

not to wear black

not to give clocks as

presents

which books to leave

unopened

drowned river

the jib *the spinnaker* *the halyard*

the free end

the shackle

end in this drowned river

valley narragansett

i learned swiftly

and forgot

the names of lines

and sails

when to step

away

when to duck

a coiled line on deck the

might catch swivel

my ankle of a boom

your body like the wind

tossing mine might buoy

a sail

some words came

later:

implosion

once a classified

term on the kitchen wall

black and white photos of

destroyers on the stems

of mushroom

your clouds

grandfather's words like still life *Life now*

paintings *became*

cached in the attic:

somewhat

difficult

because

I was

in possession of much

top-

secret

information some stories

are best

handled with care:

My decision

led to a number of absences *to take on*

the radiation monitoring

job

of several months' duration . . .

a photo of a child your uncle howard

around six *I think*

that it was particularly unfortunate

on a leash

tethered to a laundry line *With respect to Howard . . .*

his abnormal interest

in explosives

may well have originated

from

my connections *with the nuclear*

weapons program

gull haven

was the name of the house

on a wooden panel

over the fireplace

mantel

a colonial rifle once hung

your mother removed it

after

your grandfather's death   its long

thin shadow remained

the wood

around it   bleached   there was love

yes

how you cooed

a dove   once left the bough

of a spruce

to approach you on grass

looking for the other dove

there was never another dove

still

a kind of love

history

to be re- like

the blue

assembled glass

bottle

your aunt left behind

with no

instructions

numbers on the cap

embossed on glass an arrow

on the bottle's mouth

medicine i guessed

the arrow like

the hand

of a clock

would appoint the time

for the next dose

how to translate:

implosion

内爆 *nèibào*

a family

bursting in-

ward

your uncle howard

as a freshman

at harvard: *Some ill-*

advised chemical experiments

in his dormitory room

led to an explosion

and his rustication

for one year

he disappeared *Howard*

was deeply into drugs

as a user

and manufacturer

Both he and Helen

carried arms

a good bit of the time We learned

that Howard and Helen

were dead

Details

could be obtained

from Dr. Russell

in Washington

though i have left gull haven

i must ask

were there only

two bodies?

It was some relief

to know

that his tormented life

was over . . .

your cousin told of

three bodies, and a gun:

howard helen

and howard's best friend

helen's

lover?

It had been clear for some time

that there was little hope

that a most promising

and productive scientific career

could be salvaged

from the wreckage

wrought by the drugs

i look for

sails like wings

sails taut

as the skin of a

gravid belly

in the drowned river valley the lift

of my body

and drag

skin friction

against

water

a cut sail

like the wing

of

a flightless bird

reaching again

for the sky

i waded into this history

narragansett waist deep in low tide

i ran my toes

through a bed of sand

to feel the ridges of quahogs

i learned to say *quahog*

how language

at times

flows

through a diode *This is the heel of a loaf*

your grandmother pointed

as she carved it

i

could have taught you

how to count 一 *jat*[1]

in cantonese one

二 *ji*[6]

two 三 saam[1] three

「三年零八個月」

saam[1] nin[4] ling[4] baat[3] go[3] jyut[6] three years

and eight months hong kong

淪陷 fallen

leon[4] haam[6]

how japanese soldiers carved

into women

was it easier than

sliding a thin blade

into a quahog

catch them

unaware before they

clench

facing

a clear vista

of newport bridge

sails

the color of surrender

i have asked:

were the bombs

. . . this quiescent material

. . . transformed *into an incandescent*

necessary?

by the chain reaction *mass*

of incredible temperature

emitting

enormous *numbers*

of penetrating gamma rays

capable of killing

at nearly one mile . . . *During the summer of 1945*

Howard had been attending *a summer*

camp

in Virginia. *While he was away*

I was commissioned *When I went to Union Station to*

pick him up

and was in *uniform*

on his return.

he had grown *beyond recognition*

and he did not expect *a*

(necessary?) *uniform*

so we failed

to make *immediate*

contact.

. . . this

(necessary?)

transformation is accompanied

by a series of *phenomena*

that combine *to produce*

the greatest

man-made spectacle

on

Earth . . . *Finally, one boy, one*

camp counselor

and I *were left at the station.*

When I heard the counselor ask,

"Howard, *don't you see* *anyone?"*

we got together.

seagulls were

your mother's favorite birds i helped her feed them

fat and gristle skyward offerings

i turned away

when gulls circled *It was hard to believe*

around carrion

on the beach

that either Howard or Helen

were happy *with the*

life of fear

into which they had descended . . .

to be disturbed no more

either by a craving for drugs

a call from the police,

or an unanswerable

sails sharp *demand from the drug pushers*

as the trailing edge

of a wing *I make no apology*

perhaps

for what *he and they*

some may think *have found peace*

in another life

to be an

insensitive response

to a

major

tragedy

i left gull haven

expectant you tarried

with silent stories

aloft on an airfoil

trimmed the grass

cleared the attic

and watched

the sails

westbound

absolute zero concerto

there is a slight difference

in taste

between water

and heavy water the absence

of blue

blinding magnesium silver

white

flashes

almost infinite the heat

rivals the sun

peeling skin

boils like balls

firestorms ground zero

swells

with

fat blood mothers

and vomit carrying

their dead

children

smoke and

ash rise

and sweep the globe

skies

soot shrouded along the curve

to nothing

as if aiming for the absolute

perfect stillness the silence of no heat

ice over water

a year of no summer craters hollows

of

hunger and thirst

roaches scorpions

thrive

tardigrades slow steppers

renew

the hollow

of

zero

aftermath

fugue

as if the word were a note i found myself

returning to *fugue* *fugare* *refuge* *fugue* *fuga* *fugare*

to flee to chase *chace*

caccia *caccia* *caccia*

canon fettered fugue

fuga *ligata*

the canons of law measure by measure

the meter of this line the metes and bounds

of justice the farmer's wife and three blind mice

a round and around we go

i found myself returning to my neighbor's cat

who seeks refuge under my couch from bursts

of fireworks *refugio* to flee again to flee back

my mother was a refugee find me the measure of water

the rail tie marking british hong kong

from communist china

where

in this centrifuge   may

i   speak   my mind   where may i   see my family again

subterfuge   to flee under

to flee   in secret

four voices in a fugue   four fugitives

mother   father   daughter   son

four   flights   the night the cops came

was i awake?   did i see everything?

Frère Jacques   *Frère Jacques*

dormez-vous   *dormez-vous*

the night the cops came

was i awake?   did i see everything?

are you sleeping   are you sleeping

brother john   brother john

you slept through it

you were awake   you saw everything

under the canons of law

will you listen to the silence

or

the ringing

ice crystal between glass

coauthored with Maw Shein Win

an ice crystal

trapped

between

two glass panes   headed for unknown territories

inside   outside

airplane cabin   hope

cell   *l'espérance*

cage   shelter   a student refused

to take a seat   until a deportee

was removed

from the plane

disruptive zone   heartbeat   the plane   left

wait   without its prisoner

la espera

plane   arctic terns

brightness of flight   spread terse wings

across

seven continents

the prayers of sailors

coauthored with Maw Shein Win

the mekong   the mother of waters

is wide as the sea

in *cần thơ*   the plumes of egrets fall

like the sweep of bamboo

toward water   where currents converge

the mangrove roots have lost control

the house on the edge of inya lake

plumeria   snakes   sisters on piano   drops of music

a language we don't recall

strangers and pilgrims offer *guān yīn*

chocolate coins wrapped in gold paper

who do sailors pray to

in your language?

east is west   and west is east

our spherical fates

sleep by day, walk by night

coauthored with Maw Shein Win

where the mekong

begins a young monk walks

among blind soldiers

fled, flee, flew smashed butter lamps, military police

where is the middle ground?

border crossings card of rights frostbite

one who escapes the country

must sleep by day

and walk by night

water space air space current

golden stupas through clutches of trees

longitudes parallel

at the equator meet

at the poles teach me

how to read the news

without crying

a splay of feathers

you land on my back a brief
respite
from the wind
with poise
a splay of feathers
on my carapace we stand a while
rapt in the same pond
raindrops split
on the pond's skin
the rise
is slow
wet stains
on my feet my shell i peer out let
the rain
stain my scales

the wind chafes
your feathers
waves fill the sky

the wide

red pond

the endless pale

waves roil

threaten to unseat   the sand   my house

is a nest   of storms i've survived

a grooved box

you brush

your beak against

the rain recedes you unfurl

your wings

to fly   i recite

the wind   that lifts you   cloud

to cloud

my clutch

in a dune   nearby

i stay

earthbound

if i had a cousin in jerusalem

i would tell him my father used to sit

cross-legged on the floor and watch the news

in his briefs

he cried for sadat 暗殺 *ngam[3]saat[3]* enough light

to see the victim dark

enough for escape i've squeezed

into a van

with palestinian women

warm breath

in a small space here in the bay area

one student taunts another:

where's

your number? gazans

write their names on their

arms

there is no running water no time

to write last wishes

the only light comes from bombs

from fire

my chinese cousin

my jewish cousin

might hand   cigarettes

to soldiers

with the fervor

of a convert   there are weapons

enough

to light up

the world

there is a bridge

where the dead drink

and forget

so this life won't spill

into the next   cousin   if we met at

奈何橋   *nàihé qiáo*   *noi*^{6} *hokiu*^{4}

we'd forget   each other

forget

our children   we'd look

for our names

in water

we'd forget how we rolled

a ball between us laughing

letting loose frogs

in our

bellies

i've yet

to visit you in jerusalem

in the flower of cities there could be

drones

gentle as doves

smart drones

dropping digital anklets arrests

without harm

i'd like to see

olives ripen on branches

farmers harvest goats graze cousins

visit cousins

children

return and remember

composer in borrowed clothes

i hear you've been carrying

your backpack

house to house friend to friend

to friend of a friend to stranger

a different piano in every abode

in the bay

do you hear air raid sirens

in moments of silence?

do you sometimes wake up

and wonder

where you are? the young woman

who ran with her child ahead of the soldiers

the one a stranger picked up and transported to kyiv

her story

returns to me

though it's dark in hong kong the birds' whistles

have broken the day

i've been sending

african lullabies

to a sleepless friend in oakland

how to say

hush in zulu

i hope to see you

in your own clothes

playing your own piano wearing perfume

soaring like a lone seagull like the pause

before the flip

of a magician's hat

like the highest note

of a soprano

at the edge

of the clouds

ni de aquí, ni de allá/ neither from here nor there

your photo of swans

from a bridge in berlin

like white leaves

in dark waters

travel travail

trabajo travailler

somewhere between

nicaragua and the golden gate

there is

a ship fraught

with cargo *cargo, carga*

the charged showers we took

the running of your lathered hands

on my neck, back, and breasts

savor, saber, savoir

sunlight on walls in scales of gray like a sigh

watching ozu as a teenager

took you off the streets

i knew you watched ozu

before you told me *¿sabes?*

there was a pattern

on your clear shower curtain

one robot

was missing a joint

on his left elbow

that's me

you said

tell me again

your stories

in hong kong

my uncle and i would

crouch behind a railing

to watch cargo ships

load containers

forklifts and cranes

stories my mother

has yet to tell

she couldn't turn

the pages

of the music I played

on the piano

ni de aqui

ni de allá neither

from here

nor there on the top floor

of my high-rise

oakland office

we saw cranes waiting to work

poised balanced anonymous containers

to travel to other ports we knew:

managua hong kong

new york boston

we saw city hall modest and august

a wide-brimmed oak tree

in frank ogawa plaza

and the flag hoisted on a low-rise

i wanted you

to return with me

to the office at night

and watch

the lights of cars

glide up and down

the stretched gullet of broadway still

i pictured street lamps

a time lapse

photo

you would

take like

the one you

took the cathedral of

light

open still as a seashell

we said goodbye
as the elevator doors
were closing

no sabía
cómo tocarte didn't know
how to touch you

así
que te besé
la mano
so i kissed your hand

i say *de este mundo del crepúsculo*
de esta bahía de muchos
grúas y puentes
from this world
from twilight

from this bay this estuary
of many
cranes and bridges

nunca miraré la luz en la misma manera

i'll never see light

the same way

we idled

and kissed on a slope

by a stream bed i skirt

the surface

of your life

as we rose like a jesus bug

you note the shift

of the afternoon light thank you

for letting me

inside your eyes

i woke

to light shining through *oh say can you see*

your yellow curtains yes i saw

the light of the moment

as in a photo *nunca*

miraré la luz

en la misma manera

i'll never see light the same way

as when i walked on a beach

with a friend thanksgiving day

an aperture

opened

light diffracted in the clouds

and softened

the bike

on the beach *¿qué piensas?*

rather *¿qué te parece?* how does it look?

the light in my living room

¿es demasiado amarilla, no? *no, it's too bright*

not too yellow

you'd rather hide

than talk about your eyes

the eyes of a photographer you left

the civil war of nicaragua

on a standard fruit company

cargo ship your mother

appealed

to the workers on board: these are american lives

oh say can you see yours and your sisters'

not your aunt's the workers

granted passage a doctor

offered his cabin

your mother

took a more dangerous route by land

returned

to sew you shoot photos

like

a marksman to anticipate

the path of a bike down

the street

as a predator would

its prey approaching a waterhole

or gaze into

the distance

like an egret facing west

on the rocky

pacific

shore

the glass womb

a premie in a glass womb

glass   clear

and

solid   as ice   your mother couldn't touch you

empty wine bottles

in a bin

otherwise

empty

They're just glad I have a job

you, your mother and your aunt   on your pay

a photographer's pay

My mother's narcissistic

looking for a heart transplant   the twilight gleaming

behind your curtains   no

not twilight   a poet's lie

i woke to the light of dawn

filtering through your curtains   i saw twilight

when i changed my child's diapers

years ago from the hills

i watched a thin stream of light

decant over rooftops you tell me my children

come between us

i was a mother first

even as you left me

you were a mother to your mother

i thought you'd see how love flows

mother to child child to mother

i sat

at your mother's feet

once in her living room

and picked up a crumb

your aunt dropped your mother took me

into

the dining room

she'd met only one other

woman in your life they both watched closely

your mother and your aunt

as you tossed

me my jacket

before we left

not quite the ritual

of a man helping

his lover dress a point

on the arc

of tenderness let me

offer my hand

in friendship i know

the slow worried flow

of money

through a throttled pipe

you want to build

a gift for your weary self

a sugar-glass coffin

you

can climb into this glass

shatters without pain

fo^2 火 fire

loiter

on my street   i call this my street

though i moved here   only months ago—

to this monopoly board of even-sized lots

some evenings   women stand   alone   or in pairs

clothes

scant for the weather   smoking

leaning against a bike   fiddling   with a suitcase

California Penal Code 653.20: "Loiter" means to delay or linger without a lawful purpose for being on the property and for the purpose of committing a crime as opportunity may be discovered.

on whose property?   empty drink cartons

condoms behind the park bench

California Penal Code 653.20: For purposes of this chapter, the following definitions apply: (a) "Commit prostitution" means to engage in sexual conduct for money or other consideration, but does not include sexual conduct engaged in as a part of any stage performance, play, or other entertainment . . .

but this is a performance   sometimes   they lean

into car windows   sometimes   car doors open   for them

when they see me   they walk   away

a diabetic i leave my children at home

after dinner one night i take a walk

around my block—i call this my block though i didn't

grow up here

California Penal Code 653.20: (b) "Public place" means an area open to the public, or an alley, plaza, park, driveway, or parking lot, or an automobile, whether moving or not, or a building open to the general public.

a man approaches me almost blocking my way

honey! honey! he says

he thinks

i'm a sex worker arm straight, palm out

i signal as i walk: *keep your distance*

California Penal Code 653.22: (a) It is unlawful for any person to loiter in any public place with the intent to commit prostitution.

but this is a performance i circle round the block back

to my house the man reappears

from behind a tree

i have fifteen steps to gauge

if he will follow me into my house

i venture he still thinks i'm a sex worker

California Penal Code 653.22: The circumstances set forth in subdivision (b) should be considered particularly salient if they occur in an area that is known for prostitution activity.

i enter my front yard

he does not follow now

when i see women standing

on the street corner

alone or in pairs clothes scant

for the weather smoking leaning

against a bike fiddling with a suitcase

California Penal Code 553.22: No one circumstance or combination of circumstances is in itself determinative of intent. Intent must be determined based on an evaluation of the particular circumstances of each case.

i want to say i won't call the cops

i'm on your side let's share this street

they walk away i want to say come back

but this is a performance

running, running, running, working, working

in the voices of Nwe Oo, *Viet Le*, and **César Rubio**,
selected with collaborators Maw Shein Win and Julie Zhu

all experiences taught us
to be a stronger woman *running, running, running*
no matter what *working, working*

as a marginalized communities *running, running, running*
working, working

running, running, running
working, working

this is quite beautiful

all experiences taught us
to be a stronger woman
no matter what

if we don't have
that kind of experience
on my personal life
or the community's life

as a marginalized communities
we won't
be that stronger

you know the other day

as a marginalized communities

i was helping her

we won't be that stronger

bring the sewing machine

from the basement

in terms of

running, running, running,

my own discipline

working, working

i've also worked

with machines

i also work with sequence

running, running, running,

inspiration

working, working

our ancestors lived

in a tree

in a big, big tree

i had to, you know,

work every day

i was a boat refugee

a big, big tree

i don't really have

exact memories

of that

i came

a big, big tree

when i was around 3

my mom

also as a boat refugee

we escaped by boat

separately

he had taken over

our apartment

she said

oh, i really liked

your name

it's a cool name

so i hired you

for this 5-day job

we were on this boat

for about two weeks

without food and water

we run away

we run away

socialist

eventually

became a u.s. puppet regime,

initially

she worked for a woman

Mrs. Pollack she was a Polish World War II

survivor

peace and harmony

i remember disneyland

vividly

i was really impressed

with the whole maquette

we run away

we run away

is she a lap cat or a shoulder cat?

i feel like this

is who i am

and i feel like

it will never end

i was always making art

i have a solo show

coming up

major museum

in asia

in the philippines

comes and go

comes and go

she had a tattoo

on her forearm

she survived the death camp

i wouldn't call myself

a refugee now

i own a house

i have a job

i have

embodied memories

i have

embodied memories

i have

embodied memories

embodied memories

i don't feel displaced

i have
embodied memories

thinking
that was really linked
to this boat escape

i used to freak out
like i was drowning
and of course
i worked through it
and i think
when you saved me
i had . . .

we get lost

being on this small raft . . .
hijacked by pirates

they are our savior protector
they are rebel

comes and go

comes and go

we got on a ship

comes and go

initially to long beach

comes and go

comes and go

because of the lack of cargo

the company decided

people are very afraid

rowing the boat

to go up the coast

she'd usually be watching television

continuing to sew for the next day to deliver

all experiences taught us

to be a stronger woman

no matter what

dominion

Pizza *guns*

drums *music*

family *and God*

This *pretty much*

sums up *my life*

It's

a pretty good life

a bright smile almost

certainly

opened

the door *yong ae yue*

hyun jung grant

young's asian massage gold spa

it's

surreal

otherworldly 譚曉潔

tánxiǎojié 馮道友

féngdào yǒu

delaina ashley yaun gonzález

paul andre michels

soon chung park

suncha kim a really

bad

day

That's bullshit

my question to the family is

what did y'all teach him? days

a slice of strawberry before

fresh her

cream cake birthday

Ideas *as we know*

do *have*

what *consequences*

would've been

her fiftieth *that's bullshit*

I am unable

to *obtain* *I wish to stay*

my mother's *in my current home*

body *for at least* *one more*

home *month*

domicile *domos:*

house

domus:

dwelling *church* *domestic*

dam *tame* *subdue* *conquer*

domestic *dome*

half a sphere

sphere *domain* *eminent domain*

dominion: *integral domain*

absolute power

We are plagued

by ceratopogonidae

biting insects

popularly known *as no-see-ums*

because *well* *they are hard to see*

the medical examiner

around the table

they were singing

happy birthday and everyone knew

jami was dead

except her mother

They are a problem no-see-ums

so much so

that when they invade I don't simply

want

to be removed

from them

noseeums I want to smash them

hammers

godless

and materialistic noseeums

ideologies

just want to

put my mom to rest

to ask

just enough

to stay at this current

residence

at least one

while I settle more month

my mom's funeral

to rest

Here in America

to rest she did what she had to

do

the occasional slur

Nothing has happened to me

personally until now No you guys definitely

taught him some shit Take some

fucking

responsibility

robert aaron

long would stack chairs

and clean floors at crabapple

first baptist church

failed attempts

to curb his sexual urges

Pizza guns

drums music

family and God

This pretty much

sums up my life

It's

a pretty good life

2 percent

in cherokee county

hyun jung grant

譚曉潔 *tánxiǎojié*

馮道友 *féngdào yǒu*

yong ae yue

suncha kim

soon chung park

it's

surreal

otherworldly

엄마 *eomma*

i learned how to

moonwalk

because i saw her moonwalking

while vacuuming

when i was a kid

譚曉潔 *tánxiǎojié*

she worked every day

twelve hours a day *so that our family*

would have a better life

even gave me her name

世上只有媽媽好 *mom is the best in the world*

shì shàng zhí yǒu mā ma hǎo

沒媽的孩子像根草 *a motherless child*

méi mā de hái zi xiàng gēn cǎo *is like a tuft of weed*

Pizza *guns*

drums *music*

family *and God* The current battles

our churches *are facing*

require its pulpits *to be filled*

with men

who don't wear lace

on their *skinny jeans*

the medical examiner *She was a big kid*

She essentially

suncha kim *behaved like a teenager*

All my grandmother

ever wanted in life *watch her children* *body retrieval*

grandchildren *live* *the life*

she never got

which i don't want *to live*

to talk about

right now

2 percent *pure-hearted*

in cherokee county *selfless* *a fighter*

my rock

She is to remain quiet

I do not permit *Adam was formed first*

then *Eve*

naturally

more

fitted *Adam was not deceived*

but the woman was

and became a transgressor

then

I do not permit *now*

or

keep silent

fo² 火 fire

drip drop drip *Tropfen* *Tropfen* drop drip 滴 滴
滴 *dik⁶* *dik⁶* *teki* 滴 滴 滴 *gota*
dik⁶ *dī* *dī* *gota* *6/2011*
goteo PG&E
goccia goccia *$0.455* *24.1%* *quarterly cash dividend*
goutte goutte *goutte-à-goutte* *gota* drop *gota*
9/2011 drop drip drop *$0.455*
drop *quarterly cash*
Tropfen drop *24.1% dividend*
the smell before rain begins to fall and after a rainstorm
oil released petrichor
the premonition of rain
3/2012 PG&E *$0.455* *4.2%* *quarterly*
suddenly the rain *cash* *6/2012*
驟雨 驟雨 驟雨 *dividend*
zhòuyǔ *zaau⁶ jyu⁵* *shūu* *shūuuuuu*
quick as passionate flesh *$0.455* *4.1%*
rain sweeps like the hands of a harpist on strings
rain blows sideways in gusts

rain sweeps umbrellas   into sorry skeletons   *9/2012 $0.455 4.3%*

rain   can fall just enough   for dust to settle

for   the back of the hand   to feel   its weight

rain   can   hang   like   mist

霧 *mou*^{6} 霧 水 *mou*^{6} *seoi*^{2} */ wù shuǐ*

水 *shuǐ sh . . . sh . . . mist . . . ist . . . st . . .*   the slightest gauze of water

水 *shuǐ sh . . . sh . . .   12/2012 $0.455   4.5%   6/2013*

the understory   grows   *$0.455*

lush   *4.1%*   滴   滴   滴   *9/2013*

$0.455   *dik*^{6} *dik*^{6} *teki*

滴   滴 滴   *gota*

dik^{6} *dī   dī*   *goutte   goutte*   *4.4%*

a sheath of   sunlight

through the clouds   *quarterly*

12/2013   *$0.455   dddddd . . . dividend*

dddddd . . . drop   drop . . . PP . . .   *PPPPPPPPPPPPPG&E*

Tropfen   *cash*   *4.5%*

grass   in the sun's   silent   burn   *9/2014*

the rasp   of brush and bramble   *$0.455*   *4.1%*

dead trees   *3/2015*   dry

as a wasp's nest   *$0.455*   *3.5%*

dry *6/2015* as a hoarse throat

$0.455 *3.7%* hh . . . hh . . . hoarse wind sweeping the chaparral

9/2015 sweeeeeep . . . sweeeeeeep . . . *$0.455*

f . . . f . . . f . . . fēng 風 *3.5%* a draft of wind hhhh . . . hhhh . . . hhhh . . .

hhhhhhhhhhhhhoarse on brush and bramble *6/2016*

fff . . . f . . . f . . . fffffffēng 風 and the fury of fallen trees *$0.49* *3.1%*

drawth . . . hhh . . . huhhhuuuhhh . . . *hàn* 旱

drouth th . . . th . . . thhhhhhhh . . . drought kmmmm . . .

kmmmm . . . kmm . . . mmm . . . [cough] . . . [cough] . . . whoooooooo . . .

drought burns *9/2016 $0.49 3.1% 6/2017 $0.53 3.2% 9/2017 $0.53*

3.1% like the hoarse throat of the unheard

hhhhhhhoarse from screaming this earth drained

a parched riverbed a hollow beehive

hhhh . . . hhuuuuu . . . hhhhhhhhh . . . huǒ 火

hhwompf . . . fo² 火 fire and the fury of dead grass

ffffffēng 風 wind on underbrush fire *ffffffuego* *hhhhhhhhhhuǒ* 火 *fo²*

火 *le fffffffeu* *12/2017* PG&E

suspended

smoke *its quarterly cash dividend*

from a distance yān huǒ smoke soot and ash rising like a wall miles up 燒 *sssssssssiu siu*[1] searing of the skin

flames lick fur from skin

skin from flesh ashes ashes

fall

and fall a clearing

is space for thought *una pausa* to wait

is to watch

not to touch charred wood

mushrooms bloom on ashes leaves sprout

on black bark

red bird

teaches: *To*

light a fire in a

traditional way

that gives the fire power

We honor those plants

and thank them for their sacrifice Fire is alive

You give thanks to it

before you bring it

back to life again and you feed it while it's alive

You feed it and take care of it

the department of peace

Sankofa *is expressed as a mythic bird that flies forward while looking backward, with an egg symbolizing the future clutched in his mouth.*
—Rep. Barbara Lee

in the candy aisle

of a supermarket   hong kong

two kids a box of chocolates in hand   *Do you know*

where they're from?   my father asks

美國 *mei*^{5} *gwok*^{3} usa

the fine print

says   union of south africa   apartheid   boycott

black   white citizens   kept apart

prisoners

of   conscience   waiting

my brother   was   quiet   i placed

the chocolates back

mandela   曼德拉 *maan*^{6} *dak*^{1} *laai*^{1}

kept   a box of chocolates   seven months   the only treats

a prisoner got in a year

he gifted them

to a friend

my father as a teenager went hiking

with a friend in hong kong

舉手! geoi^2 sau^2 *raise your hands!*

a policeman

commanded my father refused

the policeman

let them go

when my father

told me

the story i said if you'd been a black teenager

in the states

you could've died

he agreed not that

my father could've been

a black teenager

lucille said *i didn't just happen*

to

be black

my father was black

my mother was black

i was gonna BE black

my father was chinese

my mother was chinese

i was gonna be chinese

american in madison wisconsin

my father studied the eyes

of grasshoppers dwight and my namesake bonnie

mennonite friends of my parents

chose teaching in congo over war in vietnam

9/11 barbara lee

cast a lone

vote the goddess of music is silent

in kabul zohra

splintered instruments where photos once rested ashes blow

girls hide friends cling

to the sides of planes poppies agape

the department of peace

barbara lee's peace academy

a thought

like

an egg

you're just waking up?

i dunno what to tell ya

nothing new same thing

over and over

like this treadmill i'm on it's too noisy?

ok i'll turn it off

how're you feeling? nauseous? hungover, huh?

you look like you just fell off

a roller-coaster

take a deep . . . nope

stop there's microplastics nanoplastics

in the air

like mist everywhere

smaller

than the eye can see

we're inhaling them

saharan dust can travel

thousands of miles

go back to sleep if it makes you feel better i'm getting back

on my treadmill

my treadmill's

not as fun as a roller-coaster   but it works for me

i guess you could say

i'm working for it   wanna try my treadmill?

no? oh yeah   you're still waking up.

ok   ok   i'll turn it off

guess what   i have something to tell ya

i'm gonna move

to the ocean   for some fresh air

no, not to   the water-

front

i'm gonna live   in the ocean

not as many   fireworks and guns

there

maybe the great barrier reef   swim with dugongs

apprentice with a squid

learn   how to make myself

invisible   how would i breathe

underwater?

there's ways to extract

dissolved air

from ocean water

there's microplastics in the ocean too

and nanoplastics   i know

all the way

from plankton to whales

the largest garbage patch   is four times

the area of california   the ocean

doesn't get angry   it just gets sick

my friend sean

wrote a piece of music

plastic business is the title

maybe   i should see if

sean wants to move

to the ocean   too   you've been a good housemate

don't get me wrong

sean   might find it easier

to live   in the ocean

than to eat his lunch   in his car

near oceanfront property   say

at stinson beach

how're you feeling?   still waking up?   rough morning, huh?

i mean   afternoon

you know   what's a good   home remedy

for a hangover?   apple cider   vinegar

with   warm water

don't worry about me   i'll find a clean reef

in the ocean   maybe

even clean it up a bit

with a magnetic vacuum

a place   where the water

isn't   gonna give me

an involuntary sex change

with endocrine disruptors

i wanna find

the pink

manta ray   i wanna smell

the brine   in the wind

study the genome of the ambulocetus   figure out

how i can be more like it   like

a walking whale   walking   walking

wading   swimming

we've been talking   now

almost 8 mins   8 mins and 46 secs

is a number i don't

wanna hit

i better stop

before i start crying

sean and i

have boys the same age

i don't know

what the world's gonna look like

when they're grown

well i gotta go

i'm gonna leave you

my treadmill it's yours now

i don't know about you

but i'm ready for some

peace and quiet

hope you feel better

i'll see you

where the pygmy seahorse

drifts

sorry i missed you, mike

callin' from a plane

you don't know me i know your friend

the one

you drove to vegas with

in a cowboy outfit tassles and all

fast friends

yours and mine

he told me

you could swing a bat

you could coulda

throw too been a star

you called 'im

the day he was talkin'

you died he couldn't talk

to the woman

y'all drove to vegas

he said for

i'll catch you later you tell me

if there's a later where'd

you find

those rocks

the ones

you threw   at the cops

on a   sactown

freeway?

he told me

about you in his car

over catfish and whiskey   a new flask

rice and beans

collard greens

i stopped   in tokyo on the

way back

more futons than guns   in tokyo

a coworker in oakland said futons

are the answer

wrap 'em in futons

blue cloud cloth not bullets in the back   i saw an ad in wanchai

moats of cotton

for a green burial at sea

ashes fly

Notes

Superscript numbers indicate the tones of Cantonese words.

Sound collage for "running, running, running, working, working":
https://redshadowtree.earth/file/running_working

"the department of peace" video:
https://redshadowtree.earth/file/department_of_peace

"you're just waking up?" video:
https://redshadowtree.earth/file/just_waking_up

Acknowledgments

"loiter" was performed in 2016 at the art exhibition *Resistance*, curated by Pam Ybanez for the Asian American Women Artists Association (AAWAA) at SOMArts Gallery, with performers Angela Urata and Jonathan Relucio and music by Molly Fishman.

"absolute zero concerto" was conceived as a musical performance in collaboration with Chris Chafe.

The "artographies" project initiated by Penny Edwards, with financial support from the Critical Refugee Studies Collective (CRSC), resulted in the following collaborative poems with poet Maw Shein Win: "ice crystal between glass," "the prayers of sailors" and "sleep by day, walk by night." "running, running, running, working, working" was a sound collage created in collaboration with Maw Shein Win and composer Julie Zhu, interleaving recorded narratives by Viet Le, Nwe Oo, and César Rubio. The project culminated in a live performance of the first three poems and the exhibition of the sound collage recording at the Berkeley Art Museum and Pacific Film Archive in 2018 and a performance at the Richmond Art Center in 2019.

"fo[2] 火 fire" was conceived as a musical performance for Hanneke van Proosdij, codirector of Voices of Music.

"the department of peace" was performed in October 2021 at the Sankofa Concert organized by Rebecca Nie and Jiayue Cecelia Wu at Stanford's Memorial Church. Nie was the creator of the subsequent video collaboration.

"you're just waking up?" is a video created in 2020 based on Sean Yarborough's music, with images from Paul Ocampo and video footage by Julie Zhu and Bonnie Wai-Lee Kwong, edited by Julie Zhu. The video was screened in Chris Chafe's class at Stanford: Introduction to JackTrip, CCRMA 153b Spring 2020.

Sixteen Rivers Press is a shared-work, nonprofit poetry collective dedicated to providing an alternative publishing avenue for Northern California poets. Founded in 1999 by seven writers, the press is named for the sixteen rivers that flow into San Francisco Bay.

SIXTEEN RIVERS PRESS

SAN JOAQUIN • FRESNO • CHOWCHILLA • MERCED • TUOLUMNE

STANISLAUS • CALAVERAS • BEAR • MOKELUMNE • COSUMNES

AMERICAN • YUBA • FEATHER • SACRAMENTO • NAPA • PETALUMA